Also by Charlotte Gould Warren:

Poetry

Gandhi's Lap
Dangerous Bodies

Memoir

Jumna: Sacred River

IF NOT HIM

Charlotte Gould Warren

STEPHEN F. AUSTIN STATE UNIVERSITY PRESS

IBSN: 978-1-62288-954-9
For more information contact:
Stephen F. Austin State University Press
P.O. Box 13007 SFA Station
Nacogdoches, Texas 75962
sfapress@sfasu.edu
www.sfasu.edu/sfapress
936-468-1078

Distributed by Texas A&M University Press Consortium
www.tamupress.com

Aknowledgments

I am deeply grateful to Alice Derry for her sustaining friendship over many years. Poetry brought us together and continues to animate our conversation. Derry's gift for knowing what to keep, what to cut, and why, has rescued many of my poems. Her understanding heart nurtures the work and moves it forward.

Special thanks, too, to Kate Reavey whose friendship and love of writing drew her to me. Reavey's quick mind and generous insights help clear the way for a poem to emerge.

To Sherry Bishop for her spirited take on life, and her steadying counsel, heart-felt thanks. And to neighbors, family and friends for their vital support.

To Charlotte Watts, kudos for her luminous cover photo, her work to save the land and its ducklings, and her generosity in sharing Cosmic apples, art and ideas.

Thanks to Joe Powell for his encouragement.

With love to my family—Carl, Grace, Todd, Angie, Logan and Lucas.

To editors of the following publications, my grateful acknowledgment:

Seattle Review: "How the Bunkers are Hidden"

Hawaii Review: "Apple Pie"

Crosscurrents: "Southern Hemisphere"

Washington Poets Association: "Strike the Cold Air Dead with Color"

The Madrona Project, Volume 11, Number 1: "A Time to Live and a Time To Die."

Forthcoming in *The Madrona Project* #5 "We Loved the Earth But Could Not Stay."

A special thanks to Kimberly Verhines, Director of SFA Press, for her support of poets and writers, and to Editorial Assistant, Mallory Ogea, for her quick and helpful replies to my emails. Thanks to Michael Andrews (He/Him), Graduate Editorial Assistant, for shepherding my latest revisions into the text.

CONTENTS

I Holding And Holding On

If Not Him ☙ 3
For George ☙ 4
Solstice ☙ 6
Now That You're Gone ☙ 7
Maybe It Is ☙ 8
Grief ☙ 9
We Are Never Safe ☙ 10
Bereft ☙ 11
Gritttier Than Petals ☙ 12
Poppy ☙ 13
Before I Pull Down The Blind ☙ 14
Sun ☙ 16
Walking The Dungeness Dike ☙ 17
Love You ☙ 18
Resting In A Chair, Feet Propped On The Deck Rail ☙ 19
Tell Them ☙ 21
Carrying On Like Lovers ☙ 22
Holding And Holding On ☙ 23

II River Of Time

Rice ☙ 27
Some Nights ☙ 30
Acting Tough ☙ 31
A Lesson ☙ 33
Drowning ☙ 34
Again This Year ☙ 35
What It's Like, The Girl Said, ☙ 37
Hill Station School, 1940s ☙ 38
The Poet Asks A Physicist ☙ 40
As If It Were Love ☙ 41
Snowberries ☙ 42

III Two Angels, Two Harriers

We Are Quiet Now ☞ 45
Missing You ☞ 47
Two Angels, Two Harriers ☞ 48
Fugitive ☞ 50
Even So, We Are All Destined To Vanish ☞ 51
In Full Bloom ☞ 52
Rainbow Beach ☞ 53
How The Bunkers Are Hidden ☞ 55
Buried Fragments ☞ 57
Half Moon ☞ 59

IV The Distance We Travel

"We Loved The Earth But Could Not Stay" ☞ 63
Naming The Grasses ☞ 65
July ☞ 66
Apple Pie ☞ 67
Tapping My Jacket ☞ 68
Seeds For The Jays ☞ 69
Winter Amaryllis ☞ 71
Summer ☞ 72
Hip Replacement ☞ 73
Survival ☞ 75
Asking ☞ 76
Assignment: Self-Portrait In Verse ☞ 77
Walk For Strong Bones ☞ 78
Learning To Be Ourselves ☞ 80
A Time To Live And A Time To Die ☞ 82

V Refuge

Preening ☞ 85
We Fall Off Ladders, ☞ 86
Hands On ☞ 88
Tending The Roses ☞ 89
Feeding The Horses ☞ 91
Grief In Its Fury ☞ 92
A Day For Eagles ☞ 94
Kayaker ☞ 95
Woman Without A Dog ☞ 96
Still Missing You ☞ 97
Strike The Cold Air Dead With Color ☞ 98
West Dungeness ☞ 99

About the Author ☞ 101

In memory of George F. Warren, Jr.
1934-2019

This love, this life—who could let it go?

If I defer the grief I will diminish the gift.
— "The Pomegranate," p. 216
Evan Boland's *New Collected Poems*

TWO POETS ON THE DECK

in down coats
and homemade mittens
read each other's work,
warmed by friendship.

In the mountains, fresh snow.
In the valley, already,
cherry blossoms open.

       —For Kate
         during Covid 19

I
Holding and Holding On

IF NOT HIM

Yes, I know he's gone. Yes, yes, I know
he's never coming back. But then
who is it that accompanies me—
who looks up from the kitchen counter,
opens the door when I return,
whose rough, warm face takes the chill
off mine—?

FOR GEORGE

Is there anyone as generous
and selfish
as a person in love? Wants you all
to himself.

Then is gone. Roses
to ashes.
That fast.

When had I last
lain against your chest, half asleep
with contentment?

Or held your gaze in mine,
quickened by desire?

Your shirts still
hang on their hangers the way
you undid only the top three buttons
before pulling them off over your head.

I rolled up each belt,
fitting the soft leather
into a box, coiled,
buckles gleaming,

gave your chestnut-colored
wool jacket to a neighbor
whose low blood pressure
left him feeling cold.
Days later, unexpectedly,

he walked down my driveway,
tall and slim, wearing it
as if you were back,
heart-stoppingly alive.

Your ashes settled, wind-blown,
around a young, freshly planted maple
as family circled to bless you,
poems, like prayer flags,
fluttering with tears.

You wanted us to be brave. We wanted you
to stay. We took turns at the gong you'd made
from a diver's oxygen tank,
pulling on the twine
to give it voice. Silence. And then the deep
reverberating tones, releasing you to song.

Hold the cord taut, you reminded us,
before letting go.

SOLSTICE

Moon in the autumn pine
my heart round with grief

as an oboe calling
through the dark.

What good are these last golden days
with the cold coming on?

NOW THAT YOU'RE GONE

I name each day—
Today is Tuesday.
Today is Wednesday,

wondering how swans find their way.
That year we camped in a high meadow
in full view of Blue Glacier,

their melodic gabbling
woke us at dawn.
We were like children

looking into the dark,
hearing sleigh bells.
How can I hold

such happiness
and grief in my heart
at the same time?

In the midst of winter,
swans take to the bitter air
crossing mountain ranges, salt water,

small towns sparkling with lights,
to the wind-swept tundra
where they build nests in the open.

Against all odds, I keep going too,
trying to hold on to your voice,
to the warmth of your hands,

guarding the heft of you
in my heart.
Today is Thursday.

MAYBE IT IS

Your smile in the photograph
makes it look easy.
And maybe it is. To love each other.
Maybe all those years of whacking
the tough, waist high salal with its
eager leaves so that you could triangulate
the distance accurately with a theodolite
was worth the steep climb.
Maybe rolling out dough for a pie
and changing diapers
was part of the tenderness
of the years we held each other's
hurts, discoveries, and delights,
braiding and unbraiding the riverbed of our
beginnings, the music of time
cutting through basalt until the edges
were rounded and smooth.
How is it you slipped away from me
before I could say again
how the weight of you, as you held me,
was the weight of my own heart beating,
your song in my breath.

GRIEF

What am I to do with this ring on my finger,
with the keys that freed us to come and go together?
How will I hold on to our tenderness?

Sun and moon
pull against the tide.
Clocks tick
as if to trap time.

Long ago,
when we were the evening star to each other,
you brushed my hair by the window.
I married you, a stranger, familiar as heartbeat.

Now I flail against loss
like the hapless Silver the eagle carries off.

What's heartache or hunger to the universe?

WE ARE NEVER SAFE

not even from each other
who have loved deeply.

One of us will be left behind.

BEREFT
—for George

By the time neuropathy curled your toes,
you'd lean casually against a desk
to talk with a friend, or rest
your hand on a neighbor's shoulder
to steady yourself,
rooted like the maple we planted for you.

When you hid your feelings
even from me, I'd ask you
to stand with your back against the counter,
pressing my body into yours.

You'd stroke my hair
or simply hold me,
one heartbeat, then another,
the warmth of us.

Fifty-eight years of holding each other.
Within a month, cancer had gutted you.
I think of the young tree
supple as a dancer
cut down. What's left,

scattered
like duff to the stars,
nourishing the unknown.

GRITTTIER THAN PETALS

Bruised rhododendron blossoms
fall to the grass
where ants feed on their sweetness.

I gather the petals into a wicker basket
woven by someone's hands in China,
fingers young and impatient,
or arthritic as my own.

At the edge of the ravine,
turning the basket up-side down,
I watch the petals flutter into a thicket of wind-
fallen branches a winter wren
calls home.

You're gone.
Grittier than petals, your ashes
swirl around the young maple
we planted for you—our small family—

sons and their wives, grandchildren—
drawn close against loss.

In our bedroom,
your soft flannel robe
on a peg beside mine.

All those years you and I carried each other
companionably from place to place.
I set you down now. But you are
part of the mending, part of
the loneliness I cling to
to keep you close.

POPPY

A bumblebee
climbs into
the California poppy

tipping it over—
a handbell ringing
in perfect silence.

BEFORE I PULL DOWN THE BLIND

1
Your death, Love,
sudden as a felled tree,

taking the sky with it,
crowds the window I look through

at the coming on of night.
In this mild spring air, the sky

erases itself reluctantly,
a chalky backdrop

showing off
the firs' dark silhouettes,

each twig, branch, trunk's
hard-won resilience.

2
In the fall,
I drop to my knees,

planting spring bulbs.
Then again,

with Alice in June,
summer's leafy geraniums.

Each day carries me.
Am I tethered or free?

At night, I tell you my stories,
eager to hear your voice.

Are you there, Love? I say.
You're dreaming again, I scold. *Wake up*!

I wash my face
and mop the kitchen floor.

Months later, a surgeon
replaces my ravaged hip.

I'm learning to walk again.
Grief takes time.

Neighbors, friends,
strangers, family

flare, like a blaze of wild poppies
on a sandy roadside bank

where the driver of a loaded gravel truck
waits for me to pass—

that same kind of
tenderness I hold to, for life.

SUN

on the brass
doorknob.

The heron-hunch
of grief.

WALKING THE DUNGENESS DIKE

My heart in your hand
your song in my stride
we wrap the dark around us.

Time follows the river.

Far above the shallows
the eagles' nest is bare.

Our children, our beloveds, fly away.
Fall hums in the wind
and we are small and dear.

The moon has not yet risen.

Like masts crowding a shipyard
cottonwoods sway in the wind.
Sparrows bicker and sing.

I listen to the rocking rhythms, to the pitch
and slide of the riverbank
where back-eddies ease past the current.

Our lives, one breath at a time,
mingle, working the seasons of light
into leaf-fall, renewal.

LOVE YOU

Held in your arms
nothing
was ordinary.

RESTING IN A CHAIR, FEET PROPPED ON THE DECK RAIL

1
I watch shadows of summer fog
skim over the deck. At the same time

leaves on the Clematis vine by the railing
stir drowsily, registering the current.

They quiet again
when sun burns through.

2
What are we here for,
the flowers and I,

the apple tree and the pine?
To astonish each other?

To cross over
into each other's keeping?

3
A scythe fells the field grass.
The roots hold.

The castanet-call of the kingfisher
changes little over my lifetime.

Now that I'm old, I'm no longer
in such a hurry. Did I hum

when I shook out the rugs,
when I rocked the children to sleep?

I tried too hard to be good enough.
Even so, love left its mark.

Sleep-tousled, our bare feet
traced each others' waking,

gathered sociably
under the breakfast table.

I stand quietly, now, in those footprints,
listening.

TELL THEM

Small and bright as a
hummingbird in winter

time is all we have. Whose warmth
will you reach for in the end?

Whose breath at your ear?

CARRYING ON LIKE LOVERS
—after George's sudden death

Driving home on a back-country road,
I'm startled by an eagle
swooping in like the Blue Angels over my car,
leading the way—as if you yourself
had something to do with it—
looking out for me.

I gulp back tears in the bitter air,
the salt of losing you again
blunt as the glare on unassailable wings.

That year from the deck, we watched a hooked beak
snap off a bare branch at the top of a fir,
wing-flaps ferrying the stout, long,
crooked stick right over our heads
to wedge it into a nest behind the house.

Even at night, carrying on like lovers,
the eagles' song-talk—recklessly exuberant,
pitched into the dark—
wrapped around our shoulders
like tenderness.

Are you the eagle or the messenger?

Death keeps its talons sharp,
carries us randomly as an unsuspecting
Silver plucked from the sea,
sparkling, flailing for life—just when

the heart is pierced, shudders,
and shuts down.

HOLDING AND HOLDING ON

In the willow-light of evening
when the doves have settled down
I search the world to find you
knowing you are gone.

Why have you left, who loved me,
why am I alone?
I wrapped my arms around you
against the cold.

Bright star, the sun outlives us.
Tomorrow and today, rain falls—as it will.
The doves know how to weather change.
Stay with me, help me let you go.

II

River of Time

RICE

—Jumna to Elwha

1

I come from a blazing place
in dark sunlight.

In the alleys,
hunger and anger

mingled with the scent of jasmine,
the weighted borders of saris—
scarlet, ice-blue, saffron.

My child-hands dance
to the rise and fall of rice
caught in a shallow
fan-shaped basket.

Savitri's mother
blows away the winged chaff,
quick fingers
picking out bits of stone.

We girls play house
in the shade of a feathery mimosa.

2

The sun has its own language,
eruptive, resistant,
fiercest when it flairs,

settling over our shoulders
without a sound
like wisdom.

3
Who are you, reader,
to reach across the river of time
and ferry me back?—

As if loss itself were only
a handful of petals
the deer lap up.

4
I've made my home
on the other side of the world,
in rain-shadow and salt air,
where seals haul out,
and mountains linger against the sky.

But even here, street people
hold up cardboard signs.
Blacks are crowded into prisons or shot dead
by police sworn to protect them.

We go on gathering arms.

I carry no answers,
only maps from the past
and their shadows—

children begging at train stations,
old women, dust-covered,
hauling bricks up narrow ramps,
men standing in chemicals
to tan hides for ladies' pocketbooks.

What tugs at the borders
is also undiminished—
Bits of song,
caught-glimpses of silk,

light bouncing off straw to a child's
laughter, a stranger's kindness—

all of them urgent,
waiting to be taken in.

SOME NIGHTS

the silver frying pan
of the moon
tosses its catch
to the hungry waves.

ACTING TOUGH

After weeks of sullen overcast,
sun swings, hand over hand, through the trees
like the monkeys in Allahabad
ready to spring through an open window
before the train whistle blows.

In a flash, a macaque
snatches a half-eaten sandwich
from a girl's surprised hands, while another
grabs an unguarded banana
from the cracked-leather bench
the children will sleep on at night.

We were always hungry,
everyone acting tough instead of homesick
on our way to boarding school in the Himalayas.
Six then, in my eighties now, I still wonder.
what it was all about.

Today, in the vast quiet of the Olympic mountains,
I like to imagine monkeys
pushing off from branches as they leap
from one side of the world
to the other, hooting like memory.

How would it be to live,
not knowing where I had been,
what I had lost or found? The girl in me
still cries easily for others,
but not for herself. As a child,

I had no way of knowing
my father's love
was only a way to groom me
for his predatory hands.

Now, unexpectedly,
the overcast opens up. Light
sharpens each row of raindrops
crowding branches and twigs,

slicking multiple strands
of rusted wire fencing
around my winter roses.

The shimmer and dazzle
startles me awake, just before
the train begins to roll.

A LESSON

I watched my mother's hands shaping the clay.
What would become of this small, glazed
stoneware vessel? Or of the child I was
at her side, always in the way.

This afternoon a Crossbill lights on the feeder,
its golden-brown feathers
calling me to reach for binoculars,
bringing the hooked beak close.

Cradling the spinning clay,
she drew it up
into the surprise of being,

sewed marigold-gauze curtains
for the living room window,
arranged larkspur and sweet peas
from the garden for the table.

So much was easily broken.

No one must have been there
when she was small,
needing to be held.

DROWNING

I walk through my own shallows,
shivering among broken reflections:
how you coaxed me over my head.

Too slow, too painful, this re-entry.
I run full tilt into the waves. Knowing
does not lesson the shock.

How the body adapts, rolls over, gasps
for air. I take a long breath,
pulling myself toward the pressing deep.

Salt seals my eyes. Voices of pebbles and shells
moan along the surge. Overhead,
strands of filtered light.

You'd steal into my room at dawn,
a grown man, climbing into the bed of his child.
I took to waking early, curled up,

my back to the door, pretending sleep.
It never worked. Your roving hands found me
before first light, taking what they wanted.

Now I drown in the years
of silence, gagged into telling. You said
you loved me. I lost a father.

The mother I've become storms the world,
protective, befriends the child beyond saving,
the one who wore her name—

children, everywhere, calling.

AGAIN THIS YEAR

1
Again this year
pine needles fall like rain
through summer's last, dry days.

Sailing onto skylights and deck chairs,
they catch in the rough-cropped grass,
smelling of earth and weather.

Each year, I skim off a layer,
resinous as memory,
shaking them into buckets.

With other missionary kids
I was once a six-year-old
in a Himalayan boarding school—
no money for toys.

We bunched pine needles
into make-believe sleds.

I loved scooping up armfuls of the warm
dusty needles, latching them
into a heap I could sit on.

Knees tucked under my chin,
feet dragging to slow me down,
I picked up speed, screeching
with terror and joy.

One of the older boys,
forgetting to bail out early,
shot over the edge as if
he could fly.

Ghost-pale, sprawled
far below us on a rocky ledge,

he might have been asleep, glasses
catching the sun, unbroken.

The shock of losing him, silenced me.
I too could die.

Over the years, like a body
washed up on shore,
the boy's pale throat and arms,
his quiet face, questioned me—

Why was I alive?
Why didn't I save him?

2
This side of the Pacific, the Jeffrey pine
you and I planted sixty years ago,
home to nuthatch and squirrel,
still counsels me.

When winter slicks the wooden deck,
I shake out handfuls of sun-dried needles
for traction against a fall.

A neighbor, thinking to help,
once swept them away.

3
Even as children,
that boy and I were lost,
wanting only to crowd our lives
with radiance.

WHAT IT'S LIKE, THE GIRL SAID,

to be made into sauerkraut.

They take your leaves off at the stem,
the thick wrists, the veined, delicate
spring lobes fanning out to listen.

They tear you apart from the tight form
of your overlapping
and place you in a crock.

It's cold and deep.

Vinegar and salt
rain down on you. A flat rock
presses, holding you in place.

Months, or years later, they lift the lid
to scoop you out, transparent now,
delicious.

That's what you're for, they think.
Never mind asking you
what it was like.

Or what it was like once
in the garden—drops of fresh rain to sip
from the silvery base of the leaves,

how waxy you were, new as a child,
giving off a peppery
fragrance all your own.

HILL STATION SCHOOL, 1940s

—Born in India of missionary parents, my brother and I spent five years in a Himalayan boarding school, and another six as American boarders when we returned to the States.

1
Sweaty and out of breath from the playground,
I wedge myself into the wooden desk,

jostling the bottle of ink to a shiver of light.
At six, I think with my fingers,

running them over the top of the desk to the hole
anchoring a bottle I dare not spill.

Ink, so bright, so dark on the page!
The teacher, her voice brisk,

hands out dull, grey paper, lightly scored
by wide-apart lines. We bend to the task.

2
The way an ibis drinks, I dip the steel nib
of my long-handled wooden pen carefully into the ink.

All year, laboring with stubby pencils to please her,
slant lines drawn close as wind-blown grass,

ovals, tumbling out of control like slinkies,
I hunch over my desk, diligent as rain.

Today we have ink!
Neither acrid nor sweet, its pungent smell

wakes me to the swashbuckling
sparkle of ultramarine. Drawn into a language

I will never outgrow—words introduce me
to other people's lives, to my own.

3

When the bell rings, when all the bells have rung
and all the pages been filled—even the thin, pale-blue,

stapled-in-the-center exam books of universities—
I will still feel the hunger of a child's smudged page:

No one to show it to, no one to tape it to a window—
those endless years in boarding school.

4

Today, on the other side of the world,
my eyes sting from the optometrist's dilating drops—

a bit of sun in the hall,
rain-light on the tips of the rhododendron outside.

As vision blurs, I guide one hand
with the other to write—naming the leaves, the languages

of light, wings flapping like papers my children brought home as
they stepped off the school bus—

How we gathered around the table
to discover the day's work—

tall ships in full sail
on butcher paper. Even now

those primary colors bear witness, not to history,
to that part of the child still alive in the man—

bite of salt air, creak of the mast,
how the voyage began.

THE POET ASKS A PHYSICIST

Why—today, when I walk in the quiet neighborhood at dusk,
the road surface slicked by a misting rain,
three deer browsing, lifting their heads to watch me

as I turn back, not wanting to disturb them,
side-stepping a shallow pool mirroring the sky,
a few raindrops touching down, each drop

surrounded by three concentric circles—Why
are some sets of circles larger than others?
Because the drops are heavier?

Because they travelled farther? And how,
in a dark pool,
can the circles be silver?

In India, women's arms sparkle with bracelets
as they go about their work
editing papers, consulting with patients,

patting a chapati into a stretchy circle of dough.
In the dust of grinding wheat, in the hauling of heavy bricks,
an intimate chatter of wrists companions them.

How do I explain memory's weighted borders—
the rustle of saris, raindrops chiming on the leaves of the poplar, the beat
of my heart unremarkable as the barely discernable moves of the deer?

AS IF IT WERE LOVE

Wrapped in wet newspaper for transport,
the vine maple from my mother's garden
took to our yard like any Northwest coastal native.

Fog. Dry spells. Rainbows.
When our sons stepped into the world to find
their own way, I watched the young sapling take hold.

As a child, I wanted to grow up soft-skinned and beautiful
like my mother, resinous with powders, scents,
resilience, but she never thought to protect me.

I learned, instead, like Daphne, to step inside a tree
where a father's hands could no longer find me.
Weather toughened the bark. Spring leaves turned

on their stems. The tree neither saved
nor savaged. It taught me simply
to take care of myself. How else could I shelter others?

Today, the song sparrow whets its beak on a branch.
Later, it will sing.

SNOWBERRIES

Sweeping me along
like the notes of the white crowned sparrow

and the children's voices
rising in play from Five Acre School,

snowberries
keep me moving

as I lean into the hill
learning to walk again after hip surgery,

When Beethoven grew deaf, what did he hear
but the string quartets?

I reach for the latch
of that knowing.

III

Two Angels, Two Harriers

WE ARE QUIET NOW

who used to talk boisterously
as winter wrens when we were young,

couldn't get enough of each other—
eyes, hands, mouths —

the urgency
of our hungers.

Today, with frost searing the ground,
we walk a country road

circling fields of grass
shoulder-high in sun.

You balance on old ski poles
while I coax an aching back.

We carry our small hurts with us
even in a world torn apart by guns.

Not all is lost. Here, between northwest
glaciers and the sea, a few fields,

random in their beauty, remind us
both sides of the path

bristle with wild rose and sword fern.
Around the world, people speak up, resist.

We rest together at the top of the hill,
sun in our eyes, mountains

tumbling into the sea. I pull off my mittens,
warm your icy, stubborn,

capable, un-mittened hands in my own,
the way at night

you draw me close, taking away
the ache of the world.

MISSING YOU

—while you travel in Mongolia

As the crane flies,
our thoughts

cross each other's sky,
mountains steady,

pole star high.
When you return

with the moon in your arms,
and we lie down together,

will your heartbeat
sound like the hooves

of desert ponies?
Will mine startle

like doves at the feeder?
Calling each other,

we'll explore the distance,
safe, then, and eager.

TWO ANGELS, TWO HARRIERS
—Dungeness Recreation Area

They love the sky,
these harriers, the male
calling out to his mate,

tilting and gliding
over open fields,
scooping the air

like the young lovers
we once were,
certain their gladness

mimicked our own.
He soars over her,
spring-cloud-light,

the tips of his wings
turned up as if
in expectation.

I watch them for an hour
circling higher and higher
in a dance of courtship

before they plummet, wing on wing.
Were we ever that beautiful,
that urgent? How we

loved each other!
Still do.
Why then, today,

am I spongy with tears?
Why spill them
on this bright afternoon?

I want to hear you calling,
to feel the rush of your wings
against my face, to share

the same lamp we read by
in a house we built together.
Catching me off guard,

a harsh word,
or the sting of impatience
touches ancient wounds.

Even if I could explain
what hurts,
nothing consoles

the inconsolable self
in its wanting. To love,
to be cherished.

From his perch
in the sky,
aware of every

blade of grass and its
trembling, a harrier
stoops for the catch.

Larger by a hand-span,
she's earth-toned as
woven sticks,

settling into the nest,
golden-eyed, eggs
warmed under her heartbeat.

FUGITIVE

All summer,
far from its home
in Athens,

the pressed poppy,
stayed with me,
light as a butterfly's wing,

your letter
folded in four.

EVEN SO, WE ARE ALL DESTINED TO VANISH

When the time comes,
recycle me in your thoughts.

I have loved you
as the moon

must love the dark,
or sun

the fathomless sea.
It takes a lifetime

to leave. I know only
what the heart

knows, that grief and
gladness are sisters,

that the seasons
return, and the arms

of the elder
cradle the newborn.

Beauty resists
rubble. Praise,

like light, carries us
past ourselves

into each other's
keeping.

       —for George on our fifty-fourth wedding anniversary
       27 August 2015

IN FULL BLOOM

Fireweed burns
into the green woods
of summer.

RAINBOW BEACH
 —Australia

1
I'm not sure where in the world
home is anymore.

Even in the remotest places
I find children, families
at little tables in the shade of palms,
crumbs from their sandwiches
teasing the English sparrows.

In tank tops and go-aheads,
gold chains at their throats,
young people with soft voices
order passion fruit, fish with
names like trevally,

red gurnard,
from a sea inviting
us to swim.

I imagine people's lives:
this woman in a doorway, holding
a baby to her shoulder,
waiting for the ride that takes
so long to come.

2
Sand blows up from the beach.
None of us lives unscathed.

Sea glitters its peacock colors,
waving a blue horizon just beyond
the mom and pop grocery selling

ladyfinger-bananas and yogurt.
It calls us down gritty wooden steps
canopied with shade trees and
shrieking emerald parrots,
stepping us off into loose hot sand
to pick our way through the glare.

The sea streams from the face
of a beer-bellied father
as he helps his little girl
jump through breakers, the curled
glass-green shoulders of outer waves
lifting boys upright onto boards
leashed to their ankles.

Born into the sky, they hang there
glistening and god-like just above
the roll and thunder of falling,

while friends paddle toward them
slapping the water arm-over-arm
against the weight of current.

I can feel it in the shallows,
curling around my ankles, and farther out
in the surge I swim through,
insistent, wanting to pull me past
the families, past the skittering
surfers, the shark barrier, farther
even than the unseen shelf
dropping dead away.

Everything lost and found in that
welter of waves feels like eternity,
the distant bright buoys we count on,
holding a wall of nets
against the deep.

HOW THE BUNKERS ARE HIDDEN
—Fort Warden, Washington

Even in summer, this maritime air
     draws us close. Your sweater
          wraps around my shoulders,

at home as lichen married to alder.
     Madrona and fir filter the light
          as we climb the old road.

Hidden cannons fired from here
     made history—concrete shelters
          ten feet thick, overhead tracks.

You calculate the grade of the hill,
     trucks' haul, ballast,
          what it took to protect the soldiers.

I collect pollen's fragrance, wanting us
     to share it. In such a world—
          abundance, the wash of light,

I weigh your knowledge gladly.
     Still, I want you all to myself,
          unschooled as thickets — salal,

the little-leaved Nootka rose,
     poppies, dandelions, grass so tall
          it beds itself.

We lie down too, in the upper meadow,
     warming each other, sharing
          the bedrock years of closeness,

our differences and their allowance.
        You keep counting. I watch wild sweet peas,
                their pods fuzzed and fat on the vine.

Below us, the bunkers are matted with grass,
        thimbleberry, vetch. Moss
                jambs open the great steel doors.

I think of the dead. What they died for.
        What they died of—
                yellow fever, dysentery, faulty equipment.

We're here because of them,
        our lives, like theirs, still dear and unsafe.
                In the dappled light of the leaves,

the pitch of the road, nothing has changed.
        Bees gather pollen, soon the flowers
                will set their seeds—essential grace.

You bend to gather a few wild sweet peas,
        their fragrance flaring. I think of our children,
                how years ago they dared themselves into these

under-ground chambers, echoing voices racing them back up.
        I still hear them calling, calling, as we weigh the world
        in each other's lives.

BURIED FRAGMENTS

1
How we loved our tiny rental
perched in a field overlooking
Hammersley Inlet.

Schools of mergansers
flashed their crested heads
as they dove for fish

while the salt water deepened,
blue as the chill
of a porcelain ginger jar.

Shards scattered the land
mapped for a railroad.

Lidded jars, elegantly
painted with birds and flowers,
wrapped with care in quilts by wives
for their men to take with them, far from home.

Tea steaming in bowls
to warm their hands.

They died anyway, by the hundreds,
homesick and unsung,
freezing over pickaxes and dynamite.

2
Knowing nothing, young and in love,
we'd hang our few clothes in the sun to dry.

The ginger jar, in its curving blue and white dazzle
brightened our kitchen. Until history confronted us

with the weight of anguish it carried—
shoveling dirt, splitting rocks, fourteen-hour days
in bitter weather, barely enough pay
to fill men's bellies with rice. No thanks for their labor.

Why have we not learned to bend the ledger of grief
toward compassion? Our losses shame us.

HALF MOON

Decades ago, a friend
fired a stoneware jar, the one
our children reached into
for cookies after school.

Today on the dresser, it holds
their father's ashes.

Without you, I pick up a book,
put it down, wonder
what's become of home,

gaze into the eyes of your photograph—
that smile, like the moon's.

Moon, too far out of reach
to hold in my arms,
except as radiance.

Maybe, anyway, I'd never have reeled it in—
your life ribbed like a rowboat,

the pull of your hands on the oars
stirring phosphorescence.

When stars settle on the surface of the bay,
I can touch them, but they
run through my fingers like water, like time.

All those years we shared
with our children, venturing forth
and returning, bruises and rejoicing,

the tug of our bodies
calling each other to stay.

IV

The Distance We Travel

"WE LOVED THE EARTH BUT COULD NOT STAY"
—Loren Eisley

Wherever I go,
I wonder about the trees.

How they hold
underground
in the busy dark
while carrying
sky in their branches.

They breathe
into our lungs
as if to resuscitate us
from our troubles,

branches wheeling open
like spokes
to catch the sun,

leaves shuffling and shifting
in the westerlies
before settling down
to sleep.

We cannot stay.

Each day I practice letting go,
loving what we seem most bent
on destroying—whole galaxies
of birds, rain forests,

savannas, the salt chucks
and coves of all the world's
oceans, a child's right
to breathe and be cherished.

None of us can stay.
Not the wild sweet pea
by the side of the road,
not the sailor
pulling on his oars.

Love remains.

Undeterred by time and age—
unstoppable—as if rising
out of the tight buds of the leaves
season after season.

NAMING THE GRASSES

The lovely ones run wild,
tassled, starred, burred or thistled.

Slippery as streams
the green stems gather.
A wobble of grass, a wicket.
Intimacy of pipe dreams.

I lie down with my thoughts
in a democracy of grasses.
The stroke-me grass, the be-gone grass,
stay-away stubble of brittle domain.
Cut, and cut hay.

Caught in our socks, carried
one field to another, the seed
anticipates journey—Eisley
searching in the digs.

How else
but in ignorance,
stumbling and pitching across the days,
can our lives be counted?
Red top and Ribbon grass,
Sand bur and Plume grass.

Thumbing through Hitchcock,
I discover that *"The keels may be ciliate. . . bearded
. . . or winged—"*
flight-paths of the spirit.

Quack grass, Quaking grass,
Rice, Rye and Salt grass.
Aria capillaris.
Even Little Bluestem.

JULY

Wind sweeps
dry grass
over the ears
of field mice.

APPLE PIE

I always wanted children, and my own small tree
full of blossoms,

pippins ripening under the leaves,
the fog-cold nights chased away by sun.

Gravensteins,
four or five in the grass, mornings,
a few pinched for the deer.

I have my wish. I have my work.
There, through the window,
the tree itself makes apples, year
after year.

August. September. Flour is falling.
I could dance on the floor, it's that slippery.
Children come back, grown tall.

Shaking handfuls of flour onto the counter,
I roll the dough this way and that.
Thin as paper now, my life.

Folded, lifted, patted into place, edges trimmed,
falling dough is what the cat likes—all that shortening!

The marble rolling pin, heavy and chilled,
is what the dough likes.

Speckled with cinnamon, nutmeg, lemon juice,
butter, chunks of apple.

I crimp the edges between thumb and finger,
sealing in juices, cut vents for steam to escape.
Reader, can you smell it now, the fragrance
plump as hunger—
Mukilteo, Tillamook, Saskatchewan, Schenectady?

How we gather what we love
to feed each other.

TAPPING MY JACKET

like bees
hitting the window—
first snowfall.

SEEDS FOR THE JAYS

Back then,
my children leaned into me

ate out of my hand like soft-winged
gray jays in the mountains.

Now, with lives of their own—
and sons as harum-scarum and

sweet as they once were—
strong-willed, hungry—

their arms surround me,
their unhindered talk

true as it once was.
Like you, reader,

I have stepped out
of loneliness before, and will again.

Let go of the hurt, I say to myself.
The young are needy and restless.

Sit quietly in these timeless mountains,
in the fragrant, forgetful air. Listen.

But I go on hearing the call of our
children and how they

flung the heat and weight of their
small bodies against mine for comfort,

patted my face with the flat of their hands.
Then how they quieted in my arms

and slept. I was so much a part of them
I could let go. But not this unraveling,

not my body turning wooden and foreign—
how language slides away

or hides in the throat.
I don't even know myself—

old sock, old woman.
When my grandsons call out

to paint dinosaurs and yellow suns
round as the little table they share with me,

when they tip their eager faces up
while I fasten a helmet, or read them

Goodnight Moon, I marvel,
remembering the gray jays,

their clear, whistling calls.
And how they sifted out of the trees,

one by one,
sailing in to be fed.

WINTER AMARYLLIS

What else can we give away
but ourselves?

Like children tasting raindrops,
pistils stick out their tongues.

Aren't we always stretching
to get out of the box
of one life into another,
unwrapped as rainfall?

When the lilies tip over,
I prop the container with rocks,
tie the long stems loosely
to bamboo wands.
The buds soon unfurl
into red lacquer petals.

Each day
I feel the pull of gravity,
lean into the tug
of weather and light,
learning how to fall.

The flowers remind me
that out of the difficult dark,
a sheath of life unfolds,
keeps unfolding,
asks nothing in return.

Even the fog horn,
breathing its way past shorelines,
settles into neighborhoods
quietly as silk parachutes,

while sky dreams a dancer
at the end of a green hallway.

SUMMER

Aiming
at the shuttlecock

I practice
not hitting
the butterfly.

HIP REPLACEMENT

1
Sick with the bitter taste
of pain pills,

I marvel at my walker
rolling as easily over the wood floors

as a four-year-old tumbling about
in her own abundance.

Longing to sleep in my own bed,
when I'm finally able to, the weight

of my hips and knees
torments me.

2
For the surgeon, it's all in a day's work,
sawing, separating, stanching, bonding,

suturing the body. Not nearly
that simple, of course, under the hot lights

in full view of all the instruments and human
assistants, the big clock ticking as if on watch.

3
I feel so battered and mortal, ready
at any moment to give up on myself,

although I pay strangers at Medicare
to keep me in castle-windings of paperwork,

through centuries of arrival,
to this place of redemption

where something worn out and collapsing
is replaced with titanium and ceramic, to last forever.

SURVIVAL

Even over the draw
of the waterfall's rim

stay light as a leaf.

ASKING

—with thanks to Meera Subramanian's article in *Orion*

There's a shimmer in the pines today.
Against the crush of war, a glitter
of left-behind raindrops lining every needle.

Last night I read about a woman
holding the heart of a deer in her cupped hands.
Slippery, substantial, still warm.

Men heaved the carcass onto a truck.
She took the heart home,
rinsed it in the kitchen sink,

watched the blood run dark, then pink, then clear.
As if pumping breath through the delicate valves,
she squeezed with her hands.

Open. Closed. Open. Closed.
That steady pulse
once hidden, visibly at work.

Ordinary people, neighbors, shop keepers
slung into mass graves, as if the earth could keep them warm—
child in the womb stirring, fawn in the doe's last leap.

We stumble through the rubble.
How has it come to this? And why?
For love, we say. For power.

Raindrops burnish spring branches with light.
Last night I read about a woman
steeped in many worlds.

Will someone
ever hold her heart, she asked,
in their hands?

We answer
with our lives.

ASSIGNMENT: SELF-PORTRAIT IN VERSE

Flowers sprinkled across the foreground
of Persian miniatures
crowd the borders of my dreams.
Loss clouds me. I roll like a bee
in bright transparencies.

At home on wood floors
that once were trees,
my thoughts reach out in every direction.

I am disheveled and promising
as the cherry tree loosening
its petals, or nested fawns
asleep in long spring grass.

The tight-fisted generosity
of an onion pleases me,
the glistening compartments
of an orange. I'd rather eat

than cook, read Clifton than write.
Holding a pen in my hand, still
unqualified as the child I once was,
I reach for heart's language,
complicated as a field

ticking with crickets,
red-winged blackbirds in the cattails,
the long-stemmed grasses
bristling with sun.

WALK FOR STRONG BONES

O. K., but mostly
I walk to get outside myself,

to notice how fog ruffles the cattails,
skids over snowberries, slicks

the leaves of salal before being
pushed back by sun.

Have I lived a good life—
watching over my children,

listening to the raptor-wings of their hopes,
the underground burrowing

of anger and sorrow, the sudden
sweet-grass rustle of tenderness?

Fog rushes back in, then opens
as suddenly to brushstrokes of blue.

In that field now, three horses.
At the far edge, camouflaged

by the shadow of alders,
a doe and her yearling.

Some days my body
hurts more than others—

the same path, uphill, downhill.
Every small stone

worries my bones. I huff
like a farm horse, keep moving.

Even so, I'm glad to be here,
walking in fog and sunlight,

linked to the earth,
to Navajo runners, Masai warriors,

caribou crossing the barrens, guarding
their young. The great

bow is bent. The body has its reasons,
the mind its unrestricted heart.

LEARNING TO BE OURSELVES
—Eighty-five

Am I going to stay in bed all day?

An orchid, an amaryllis,
fir trees against a quiet sky
look back at me, warmed under a quilt.

Not that I didn't love him
or the children

born of such tenderness
they seemed invincible, devouring us
with their hungers

before the deep sleep
of contentment.

We become each other's
stories, calling out through the years
no matter the wounds.

I teach them how to
lace a shoe, to find the water-strider,
delicate as an eyelash, scribbling
its way across the current.
They teach me who I am.

Even now, a great horned owl
calls from the madrona,

where under the quilt
all four of us, momentarily
together in the great wide bed,
quit whispering to listen.

These days—except for my body—
the bed is empty, and full of conversation.

Whether I'm lonely
or not, in the shadow of maple leaves,
cones still drop from the fir.

A lashing wind and rain
quiets to radiance.

A TIME TO LIVE AND A TIME TO DIE

My time now
is a time to die. Not at once, but soon.
I'm grateful for this house
warm and full of light,
our children's voices like hand-prints
covering the walls of my heart.

The ragged edges of getting along,
the sweet moments of closeness, all of us
pitching in to hoist a canoe to the top of the car,
remembering the paddles, the sandwiches, life jackets,

and how at last we hauled our craft
over the hummocks of sand-grass
into the pebbly shallows, pant-legs rolled up, one foot,
then another shaking the water off, getting inside,
pushing off, afloat. That holy silence. Seawater

sliding off the paddles, salt air and sun
opening the sky around us.

Or how, in the Fall, the geese call us out, their wavering vee's.
How we lie on our backs in the dark, talking quietly,
waiting for the Perseid showers to scatter the sky.

This house, these loves, I must let them go.
The moon's lantern in the Douglas fir,
the Cooper's hawk settled on the railing,
butterflies, rainbows.

Why was I so often sad in the midst of all this glory? As if
the world was broken and I couldn't mend it? As if I myself
would never mend, when mountains rise and fall,
and the sea itself unravels its shores. Love endures.

I give you mine. I hold yours.

V

Refuge

PREENING

its light-struck feathers,
a swallow balances on the telephone wire,

the flow of conversation
under its feet inaudible.

Maybe in just this way,
we cannot know God.

WE FALL OFF LADDERS,
—for Charlotte Watts

fall in love.

Some days the sky
looks so blue
even the first snow

fluttering its great wings,
settles down.

The blind child
sees with her ears, the lost child
rescues others.

Learning to sing helps.

A woman I did not know,
whose voice I heard over the phone,
mended some part of me

I hadn't noticed was torn.

Beethoven had so much energy
he kept having to
get out of his own way.

Music helps:

feeding us with its
dove-grey shoulders,
its pink feet a surprise
we hold still for like a child.

Or the great kettling up
of hundreds of thousands of
Sandhill cranes as they

call to each other
from the corn fields of Nebraska.

At night,
in the meandering shallows
and interconnected islands
of the Platt, they'll sleep,

taking refuge from predators
before heading south.

Knowing helps.

Most of the mysteries
are right in front of us.

Inside the red tulip,
black,
and a splash of yellow.

HANDS ON
—for Lynette

If I could be as ready to assist
as hands are. If I could grip
and not let go, and then
when the time comes,
let go generously as the wild rose
its over-lapping petals.

At Sunny Farms—
all of us wearing masks—
I'm picking out mushrooms,
surprised to hear my name.
A woman's eyes meet mine.

I knew her as a girl—shy, quick to grin.
Here she is, lovely and tall,
weathered as I am,
a pediatric nurse
with three grown daughters of her own.

George died last year, I say. Her hand
flies to her heart like a gun-shot bird,
eyes above the mask
urgent with care. The way the left hand
comforts the right, and the right
folds into it.

At the check-out stand
I hear her greet another friend, her laugh
hearty, enduring—one hand
gathering up the groceries, the other
easing aside a lock of hair.

TENDING THE ROSES
—for George Floyd

In the bending, the reaching and lifting,
the coupling of a hose, its dragging weight,
the cool spray of water,

what rises up in her,
gnaws on the neck bones,
the lower vertebrae, the vulnerable knee.

It is all she can do, an hour later,
to put away the tools, ancient
leather gloves in the shape of her hands,
clippers for Black Spot and Leaf Curl,
the long-handled draw of four curved tines
she uses to pick up the hose, again and again,
without bending. None of it
keeps the lion from its kill.

Pain. Invisible as time.

Three white policeman watch a fourth
kneel on the neck of a hand-cuffed black man
who gasps, I can't breathe. Even a stranger's camera
recording his innocence doesn't save him.

And if it were her neck,
or the neck of America itself being kneeled on,
would anybody mourn?

Caught in the snare of history,
her own pain is fugitive.
She longs to join the marchers,

bends, instead, to the task at hand,
unlaces her gardening shoes,
steps awkwardly out of dusty
pull-on pants, lifts everything that hurts

into bed, tugging sunlight and the cold chill
of covers over her shoulders.

FEEDING THE HORSES
—For Lisa, Lynn & Mark

They whinny softly by the corner bedroom,
meaning to wake us. Not yet morning,
pitch black, Montana, ten below.

Still warm from sleep in your hand-built house,
my body senses its way beyond the clearing:
two hundred acres of hardwood and conifers
turning to stars.

The horses follow like shaggy dogs,
snow on their backs. I finger the dark
as if it were Braille. First the shed takes shape,
then rope, harness, shoes, the long, smooth
handle of pitchfork. Horse hooves
quicken, jockey for position.

On curving steel tines, I gather a weighty thatch-work
of summer hay, shake it loose,
the sound of falling like darkness settling,
or the promise of love.

It's a walking gait—a trust in the daily
we dare not take for granted that keeps us
from anarchy: seedy stems on boney jaws,
the munching and grinding, whispering and
falling, the soothing retrievals—
smell of sweet hay.

By dawn, I can guess two shadowy forms
as if they were poems:

stars full of ears,
rumps lost in a thicket of trees.

GRIEF IN ITS FURY
—for Llynn Wicklund

Fog blows through the apple tree and the Big-leaf maple,
summer fields undone.

From the Strait of Juan de Fuca, ships' horns moan,
probing for shore.

I sit on the deck of our house in the lee of the wind,
badgering death—

Why must you go first, Lynn? Why don't I?
The exuberant reds of geraniums I planted last spring

startle me now, their colors brash.
When the top of a Doug fir snapped off in a storm

decades ago, a new leader took hold.
Today it curves upwards, thick as a man's waist, trunk to sky,

shaggy with needles. Into the crook of that arm,
eagles ferry sticks, as if to console with precarious building.

Against time itself. Tattered as a spawning Coho,
you still reach out to others, give away what you can.

You tell me about days edged with the effort
to get things done, cavernous nights.

Pain wraps you this morning, thick as wet sheets.
Taking turns, each of your four boys leave their jobs

to visit for a week, one story leading to laughter, another
to sobs. They bring flowers, clean gutters, fix a door lock,

help you buy a recliner when you can't get out of bed,
one that tips you up onto your feet to reach the walker.

They wrap their big arms around you
wanting only to be held.

A DAY FOR EAGLES

Syria! Why have we abandoned you?

So many lives
turned to death and rubble,
treasures smashed—
while I walk the bluff trail,

while I catch the high, chipping call
from the north as an eagle sweeps by,
wings held flat, snowy head blazing.

First, its downward gliding spiral
toward the Strait. Then a partner
mimicking each turn, each leisurely
figure-eight as they swing back toward me
to ride the up-draft north.

My heart aches for fathers
carrying prayer rugs, cook pots,
bedding. For mothers
slung with coats and children
struggling toward an unknown border.

Their voices cry out as I return home
in the last of the sun, while robins
and Stellar jays gather, and the fallen

walnut-and-honey-colored pine needles
catch, like children's kite string, in the gutters.

KAYAKER

—for Chris Duff circumnavigating New Zealand's South Island

I think of the lone kayaker
pushing his way through piling up
seas as he rounds
another headland. Months
of solo paddling,

How we pitch ourselves
over the edge, or are thrown.
Chance, or a lifetime of training
rolls us over alive, keeps us
gasping as the bright salt water
of the world falls away.

Is it our hands
that pull us forward, drenched
and buoyant over unknown ground?

Not until we make our final landing,
peel out of whatever harness
sustains us, do we find ourselves surprised
by the fragrance of wild rose in the thickets,
bunched and nameless grasses,
our own lives bone-tired and somehow
not yet banished
from what we hold most dear.

WOMAN WITHOUT A DOG

A woman with white hair
walks under the cherry trees on 5th street

as if she were carrying off
a cluster of petals to the small upstairs

apartment where a blue vase of sky
waits at her window.

When I turn the corner, she's gone,
taking me with her.

She hasn't seen herself under the spring trees
Monet might have painted,

or how she lingers through the years
as if to say, all three of us are in this together,

crowding the frame,
the sky astonished as ever.

STILL MISSING YOU

Little windflowers
rising through the grass
around the apple tree's

moss-covered trunk
surprise me each spring
their shimmer of blue.

As young lovers, you and I made our way
across shale-cut
slopes in the Olympics

to an alpine lake
the same clarion color,
water achingly cold.

Soon sparkling
through our fingers
it ran quick-silver clear.

Only when we stepped back
did the lake retrieve
its sky-blue sheen.

Basalt peaks tattered with clouds,
the mossy snows of summer
mirrored upside down.

Alone now, all around me
the world stays deeply rooted—
as we were—loving

and being loved, surprised
by the song of the horned lark
rising from meadow grass.

STRIKE THE COLD AIR DEAD WITH COLOR

October has the brightest air; it stokes
our lives. Pelted by rain, stones ignite,
colors catch fire, a bolt of wind provokes
the yard, scattering branches in its bite.

Give up the darkening trail, for river's run.
It prances like the leaves, invites our play.
The cutthroat lies in shadows tagged by sun
to spawn its leap, and shake against decay.

We hunt for tender roads that woods repair.
Rot feeds the great up-lifted trees to gold.
The leaves know how to travel light and spare;
their feisty affirmation turns the cold.

So, teach our love to burn against despair.
Before we drown in earth, we'll dance in air.

WEST DUNGENESS

Slowly, slowly
the hardwoods tender their leaves
while my heart opens to neighbors' kindness.

Joe hauls my garbage bins.
Donne' and Craig help me move the bed.

As the sap rises, as the air softens to sun,
wild current blooms, hummingbirds return.
The tightly-wrapped buds of alder and maples
unfold into their becoming.

I can hardly keep my eyes on the road.
Even the evergreens look astonished
before this world of sky-rivers and ravens.

Unfurling bright transparencies—
green-gold, viridian, fugitive—leaves
tumble up into the sky like school children
onto the playground.

Today I've been planting geraniums.
They teach me to breathe, urge me
to reach out to others, where the tangled
filaments of our lives nourish and take hold.

A little girl on her swing
pumps the air with her legs, sailing higher and higher.
She is five, maybe six.

I look for her—and she's almost always there
by the corner of Nelson road—head tilted back,
feet to the sky,

my own child-hands hanging on
past fear for the thrill of the ride.

CHARLOTTE GOULD WARREN is the author of three poetry collections, *If Not Him*, SFA Press, *Dangerous Bodies* (SFA Press), and *Gandhi's Lap*, winner of the Washington Prize in D.C. (Word Works). A memoir, *Jumna: Sacred River* (SFA Press) chronicles her childhood in India during its fight for independence, and her coming of age in the United States through the turbulent sixties. She earned her MFA in Writing from Vermont College, taught part time at Peninsula College in Washington State. Her poems have appeared in *Calyx, Orion, Hawai'i Review, The Louisville Review, Kansas Quarterly* and other journals, as well as on Seattle buses. She and her late husband have called the Olympic Peninsula home for over fifty years. Its many rivers, mountains and inland sea continue to inspire her. As the seasons change, swans fatten up in Nash's fields before heading north to nest in the tundra. Huckleberries ripen and salmon return to their spawning grounds. In the high country, the call of bugling elk. Warren also treasures her family—two sons, two daughters-in-law and two grandchildren—as well as a vibrant community of friends.

Printed in the USA
CPSIA information can be obtained
at www.ICGtesting.com
JSHW022157110923
48293JS00011B/111